Experiences in the Southwest:

The Sharecropper's Son, Part II

by

Samuel Smith, Jr.

authorHOUSE®

AuthorHouse™
1663 Liberty Drive
Bloomington, IN 47403
www.authorhouse.com
Phone: 1-800-839-8640

First published by AuthorHouse 2/16/2010

ISBN: 978-1-4490-3905-9 (e)
ISBN: 978-1-4490-3906-6 (sc)

Printed in the United States of America
Bloomington, Indiana

This book is printed on acid-free paper.

Special Thanks

I owe a special thanks to my wife, Thelma Howard Smith, for her patience and encouragement and to Jamie Popejoy Aguilar, for her typing and computer expertise. Added to these faithful individuals are other dear friends: Gilbert and Sylvia Zapata and Michael Otondo.

Introduction

In June of 1974, with much consideration and with my doctor's advice, I relocated from the northeast to Tucson, Arizona, with my son, Leumas J. Smith, and his mother. Betsy, my 1965 Plymouth Valiant (the slant six), was packed and loaded with our belongings, with enough passenger space left over for the three of us. On the eighth of June, I arrived at the University of Arizona's student housing on Columbus Boulevard, near Rillito River. Resettlement in the Southwest somewhat severed family ties for my child. I knew that my son would not have the opportunity to grow up near any of his paternal and maternal relatives and other extended family members. Le (our only child) was just two years old when we moved from Newburgh, New York and established permanent residence in Tucson. In that same year, Le turned three years old. He would not grow up around the family. So, whether it is intentional or not, the lack of proximity (in the minds of some relatives) is a root of distrust toward those relatives they seldom see.

Table of Contents

Introduction.. v

Chapter 1: Unforeseen Circumstances.......... 1

Chapter 2: Intrastate Relocation................. 21

Chapter 3: A Neophyte in Action............... 23

Chapter 4: Graduate School:
Learning How to Learn............. 37

Chapter 5: The Ugly Head of Racism......... 55

Chapter 6: An Educator's Perspective
on Education 59

Chapter 7: A Father's Son............................ 67

Chapter 8: The Hatchet Era 77

Chapter 9: Enough...................................... 89

Chapter 10: People of Influence 93

Chapter 11: A Reflection............................. 103

Chapter 12: My Mother's Final Days:
A Transition 105

Chapter 1

Unforeseen Circumstances

Unforeseen circumstances were what I faced in the office of the University of Arizona's student housing. The office secretary stated that there was no apartment available and that a local minister in Tucson had alerted the office that I would not be coming to Tucson to attend the University of Arizona. This was disappointing news on that morning. In response to the office manager and his secretary, I stated that I had not been in contact with any local minister or any person to act on my behalf for an apartment in student housing. How this mistake happened is beyond my comprehension. Immediately, I called the local minister, whose name the office released to me, and reported to him what the office had said he had done. He denied everything. He emphatically said that he never called the office. Yet, the University of Arizona's student housing had the local minister's name and telephone message associated with my application for an apartment. Today, I still question that local pastor's honesty.

Having learned that someone had finagled me and my family out of an apartment was like a fifth columnist who had sabotaged and robbed me and my family of domestic comfort. Such interference led me to seek shelter in a motel. It also imposed further economic burden and hardship upon me.

The motel in which we resided was on the south side of Miracle Mile, near what used to be a semi-circle intersection. On the north side of Miracle Mile, opposite the motel, was a cemetery of several acres with a mortuary. We occupied a very small room with a kitchenette. The space within the room was limited and very inconvenient. But the three of us survived in that small room for more than a month, until an apartment became available at the University of Arizona's Student Housing.

A Visit to the Financial Aid Office Registration and Course Selection, Issues that Govern Life

To determine whether I had been approved for a grant, I decided to visit the office in person and inquire. As it was, I had already submitted an application for financial aid to attend the University of Arizona well before I left the northeast. Initially, the reception I received in the office was not a pleasant one. The words I heard were rough and without tact.

Brother Ivory, a Black American, addressed me with words that were like the trail of combustible wildfire. He said, "What makes you think you ought to get a grant?"

Not knowing what to say after hearing those startling words, I replied, "Because I have a family and want to go to school full time."

Brother Ivory then asked, "Did you file an application for financial aid?"

"Yes," I replied.

He then walked to a place where there was a large stack of papers. He looked at me and said, "I cannot find it. Come back tomorrow."

I went away thinking and saying to myself that I would have done better meeting and conversing with an Anglo American. At least he or she would have better understanding and some empathy for my plight.

The next day, I returned to the financial aid office. Brother Ivory was still communicating to me with words that had the sound of crackly, snapping fire. He said, "I am going to get you a grant! Do not be like these other black students who hang out in the student union and fail. Get help before it is too late. You are probably going to find that the University of Arizona is harder than Orange County Community College in California."

I made an effort to correct what he said. I said, "It is Orange County Community College in Middletown, New York and—"

Before I could finish, Brother Ivory said, "Whatever!"

I was exhilarated when Brother Ivory informed me that he would get me a grant to go to school! Now, I could go to school full time without being interrupted with the economic burden of supporting my family. Another thing concerning Brother Ivory was now apparent: once I had braved his roughness and whirlpool of fire, he became the instrumental channel which providence used to procure financial aid for me. At the conclusion of our talk, Brother Ivory instructed me to go to the registrar's office. A specific lady in the registrar's office informed me that the university would need my high school transcript. I had already submitted the transcript from the community college I attended in the Northeast. I was unaware that one needed to submit a high school transcript upon completing a two-year college. This matter was resolved without any difficulty.

In the course of time, Brother Ivory and I struck an amiable compromise. While I was going about the business of my studies on campus, Brother Ivory joined me and asked, "How are you doing?"

"Ivory," I replied, "I am just trying to keep my head above the water."

"You are doing better than that," Brother Ivory said. "You have a 3.75 grade point average!"

"Is that what you do? Look at the students' grade point averages?" I responded.

Brother Ivory replied, "Sometimes. You almost have a 4.0 GPA. Next semester, I am going to get you a scholarship. You must maintain a 3.0 GPA and above. I will give you the name and address of the person affording the scholarship. I want you to write the individual and thank her."

And this I did.

On another note, Brother Ivory personally invited me to attend his place of worship. I was obliged and gladly accepted his invitation with a heart of gratitude.

A University Attendee on the Horizon of Life's Issues

Prior to the commencement of the autumn semester registration, I was told about the horror of registering under the hot Arizona sun. The individuals who shared this information were boiling with the voice of negativism. They said that many students fainted, because of heat exhaustion from standing and waiting to register under the Arizona desert sun. These negative individuals also said that many classes that I needed would be closed, since I would be a first-time registrant at the university. Come what may, none of this dissuaded me. I was even more determined to attend school and earn a bachelor's degree. No one could stop me! No, not even a pair of oxen like those my grandfather Smith once owned!

All anxieties concerning my first-semester registration ceased, thanks to one Robert Smith. At that time, if I recall correctly, Robert was a senior who was already enrolled. (If not, he was a graduate student.) Robert quietly came to me and asked if I would work registration. I immediately seized upon this opportunity and worked for four semesters. Although Robert and I were not related, he befriended me at a most opportune time.

Early on the morning of student registration, I reported to Bear Down Gymnasium as Robert had directed me. Robert's superior established my identity. He then gave me my registration packet and directed me to the McKale Center. Consequently, Robert's kind heart and concern enabled me to enroll in all the classes of my choice. Registration was accomplished smoothly and without any difficulty. None of the classes that I needed were closed. What silenced the negative individuals was that Divine favor was upon me throughout the entire process of student registration.

In the early 1970s, I had plans of becoming a sociologist. I disclosed this to two college professors: Dr. Burns taught sociology at Orange County College in Middletown, New York; the Professor (I do not recall his name.) had his PhD and taught sociology at the University of Arizona. These two professors did not know each other. Neither did I discuss with each what the other had said. Each professor said that there was hardly any demand for employment in the field of sociology. For this reason, I chose to pursue a career in the field of secondary education. After much consideration, I specialized in social science (also known as social studies).

On the home front, Le was increasing in stature. He was learning to play with the other young children in the neighborhood. Many times, he would venture a few yards from our apartment and gather where the other small children were gathered. Le was a brilliant child. He was eager to learn and quick-witted. Active and agile, he was energetic and had an excellent attention span.

A fellow student in one of my political science classes asked me if I had a son named Le. I said that I did. She emphatically said that Le did not know how to share. I then replied, "What child two or three years old knows how to share?"

This female colleague responded, "He cannot do anything wrong!"

"That's right," I said.

After hearing those infamous words, I knew that troubled waters were on the horizon. Sometime later, Le's mother said that someone had complained about Le meeting and gathering with the preschool children. It appeared that someone simply did not want Le to attend preschool.

Because of my tenacity, Le continued attending, and I informed his mother not to stop him. In addition to the home environment, preschool was another environment where Le could experience early childhood training, learning, and meaningful activities.

The preschool system's reaction to my decision resulted in a call from the social worker. The social worker's indictment was that Le was being neglected. I assured the social worker that Le was not being neglected. I pointed out that the underlining basis of such a complaint was that I permitted Le to attend preschool and refused to stop him. I further stated that many white Americans say that black people do not want to attend school or learn or do anything.

"Here is a child," I said, "who knows nothing about racism. He is interested in learning, and you do not want him to attend because of racism. School is the place where Le should be."

Of course, the social worker disputed my charge of racism and said that my decision to allow Le to attend were factors that lead to that contemptuous complaint. All of this happened on a day when I had just arrived from school. As if I did not have enough problems and concerns, now I had to contend with the aforementioned smear tactics.

In spite of these contentions and careless remarks made by the social worker, a ray of hope surfaced. The next semester, Le and a Mexican-American child were awarded scholarships to attend preschool. Now the system legitimized the right for these two ethnic/minority children to attend preschool. As a result, Le and the Mexican-American child attended preschool for four semesters and received scholarships for the last three.

As an undergraduate student, I spent countless hours attending classes, studying and reading, writing papers upon papers, doing research, doing other assignments, and participating in a student work-study program. At the close of the day, I was ready for a brief break, and I looked forward to going home. Each day, Le would roll out the welcoming carpet for me as if I were a dignitary. He would come vigorously running to greet me with hearty smiles and pleasantries. I would lift him into my arms and say, "How is Daddy's boy?" As it was, Le was indeed the epitome of enthusiasm and the beloved son of his father. In addition, the young fellow was brave and dauntless.

Student housing was a very convenient place to live. The grounds were well kept and maintained. The lawn and hedges were always manicured and the picturesque mountains and hills that sat to the north further enhanced the view. Play areas were available for the children and for adult sports activities. One could study for unending hours because of the availability of study rooms. The parking facilities were more than adequate. One also had easy access to the city's public transportation system. If I recall correctly, Tucson's bus system was known as the Metro-Tram. Sometimes I would ride the bus to school, especially when I was not willing to face six miles of traffic to and from the university.

Another option was that students could rent a small garden plot for a minimal fee of $2.00 per semester. I rented a garden plot for four semesters between 1974 and 1976. Aside from the benefit of homegrown vegetables, gardening was one of the ways in which I could relieve stress and frustration. It allowed me the chance to exercise, relax, and ponder.

From my perspective, living as a resident at student housing was paradise. I once said that I could have lived there for the rest of my natural life. But I knew that this was not feasible. One had to move onward after graduating from the university.

As it does for a foot soldier, time progressively marched onward. Soon I was a senior who had made every effort to extract what knowledge was being afforded. Yes, some of the classes were extremely challenging. For example, one of my classes had an enrollment of more than four hundred students. Another class required the perusal of eleven books, along with extensive research. A part of that research was on microfiche. Still another class required students to establish a placement file. Included in the placement file were three references from various individuals, one's cultural background and origin of nativity, one's work history and work experience, and one's professional career academic major.

Eyewitness accounts and hands-on experiences were an integral part of the education major's curriculum. Many students became acquainted with the surrounding public school systems in the vicinity of Tucson. We students observed various teaching methods and styles of certified public schoolteachers. This was exceedingly helpful. One could determine whether he or she was best suited to teach grade levels seven through eight (junior high students) or grade levels nine through twelve (high school students). I quickly realized that I was more inclined to teach high school students.

The practicum was another hands-on educational experience. This pragmatic experience featured an educational adviser from the university and high school levels. One could now make a decisive choice to execute his student teaching at one of the neighboring schools. I chose to perform student teaching at Tucson High School during the last semester of my studies.

Much time was devoted to learning the art, ideology, and intricacies of teaching. Added to this, each student teacher was required to develop appropriate lesson plans and to state goals and objectives.

Thanks to the university adviser and the regular classroom teacher under whom I had performed student teaching, I satisfactorily completed all the requirements in 1976. I continued student teaching at Tucson High School until their school year was completed. The day of recognition came when I had received a bachelor of arts degree in secondary education. From my viewpoint, this milestone was a family accomplishment. Consequently, a photograph was arranged for the entire family. This portrait featured Le and his mother and the graduate in uniform. Le sported his father's cap and held his father's degree. In addition, essential credentials were procured from the university's college of education and hurried to the state department of education in Phoenix.

I was issued a valid teaching certificate for grades seven through twelve. For greater employable accessibility, I filed a copy of my teacher's certificate with the Pima County School superintendent in Tucson.

The conclusion of two years of undergraduate studies was imminent. In contrast, my need to work was ongoing. I was doing maintenance in a work-study program when I received a call from the placement office sometime in May of 1976. I was asked if I would like to come to the office for an interview. I gladly accepted a 3:00 PM appointment, simply because I did not want to lose that much time from work. When I arrived at the office, the principal of Kofa High School (Yuma, Arizona) was waiting. He asked me a few easy-answer questions.

"How did you get from North Carolina to New York and from New York to Arizona?" he asked.

"I had to continue relocating to improve my living conditions," I replied.

"Have you ever been to Yuma?"

"No," I answered.

"Yuma is largely an agricultural community. I notice that you are a minister. Will that interfere with your teaching?"

"No, our services are held at night and in the evenings," I explained.

"If you get a job teaching in Yuma, will you move to Yuma?"

"Yes."

"We are going to send all of our applicants an

application. When you get yours, fill it out and send it in right away. I cannot say you will get the job, but I will recommend you," he said.

As the principal promised, several days after the interview, I received an application from Yuma Union High School District #70. What I mostly recalled concerning the application was my philosophical view on education and how I would best motivate students to learn. Upon completion, the application was placed in the mail and forwarded to the district. Shortly after that, I received a call from the principal's office of Yuma High. The principal's secretary requested that I come to the school for an interview. She also mentioned that only one other person was selected for the social studies position. "That ought to tell you something," she replied. She politely asked if I had ever been to Yuma.

"No," I said.

Afterward, the secretary furnished me with directions to travel from Tucson to Yuma. Also, I was told to exit from Interstate 8 onto the Sixteenth Street exit. At that time, anyone who traveled from east to west on Interstate 8 had to exit onto the Sixteenth Street exit because there was no other exit beyond that point.

At the appointed time, I arrived at Yuma High School with my family. I was interviewed by a trio: the principal, the assistant principal, and the head of the social studies department. When I first observed these three men, I cast a stereotypical notion upon them: *These men are going to roast me. They will ask me questions that I do now know,* I thought. Nothing could have been further from the truth, not even the distance that the east is from the west. These men were cordial and considerate. According to my recollection, the principal asked if I belonged to any professional organizations. At that time, I was a member of Kappa Delta Pi. Repeatedly, the assistant principal kept saying, "We want you to teach the kids something."

My son Le kept walking in and out of the office while the interview was in progress. His busy walk-through observations did not seem to bother the trio. I made an apology for his action, but the trio assured me that Le's busy movements did not bother them. One of the men asked if I would like to have a cup of coffee. Le boldly shouted, "My daddy does not drink coffee!" His canny saying moved everyone to hearty laughter.

An important issue was raised during the interview. I asked the trio if they would require me to cut my hair. In those days, the afro hairstyle was very popular, and I wore one to express my ethnic identity. The assistant principal said no. "If anyone is going to be concerned or worried about hair," he said, "that person does not need to be in the teaching profession."

The assistant principal went on to say, "We want you to dress in a manner that will not distract the students from learning."

Surprisingly, once phase one of the interview had ended, the principal said, "I am going to take you to meet the superintendent of the district." I had no prior knowledge that phase two of the interview had been arranged. The superintendent of the district would also interview me! The superintendent received me with open arms. He appeared to be a superintendent who genuinely cared about the well-being of his teachers and of those individuals who were under his authority. As I perceived that employment was at hand, I presented issues to him. "It is expensive to move from Tucson to Yuma? How do I know whether I will have a job next year or not?" I said.

"Sam, based on the references that are before me, you will not have any trouble here. You will have to mess up really bad not to have a job next year," the superintendent replied.

As planned, once the interviewing was completed, I decided to take a few days of leisure from the arduous tasks. My family and I continued traveling west from Yuma via Interstate 8 on to San Diego, California. Just west of El Centro, California, as we were rolling on the horizon, I heard a loud noise from the right rear of Betsy, my car. Not stopping to investigate what was wrong, I continued traveling through the fascinating desert and the scenic mountains to San Diego. The next morning, I took Betsy to the automotive shop. There the mechanic noticed that Betsy had blown a right rear axle bearing.

This was our first time in Southern California and Betsy's first repair work in the same region. Aside from the repair work on the car, most of the day was spent at the San Diego Zoo. The San Diego Zoo was quite an interesting place for entertainment and recreation, an escape into the diverse world of animals, and firsthand knowledge of their realms.

From San Diego, we traveled north on the western Pacific scenic route into Orange County. There we toured Disneyland, the largest amusement park that I had ever visited! Disneyland was a conglomeration of themes that portrayed the cultural, social, and historical contexts of American society. Interestingly, I first heard about Walt Disney and his Disneyland during my early teenage years. Since I'd grown up in rural eastern North Carolina, Walt Disney's amusement park was many miles away! Never did I dream that one day I would set foot on its premises. Now that I was standing in Disneyland, its various attractions were exciting. They far exceeded my imagination and expectations! Though I was an adult, my childlike exhilaration emerged, just like my son's.

Our day of pleasure and leisure ended, leaving us with pleasant memories. We returned to Tucson, and within a few days, I received a teaching contract for 1976 to 1977 from Yuma Union High School District #70. I signed and dated the contract and returned it to the district.

Chapter 2

Intrastate Relocation

In July of 1976, we returned to Yuma to find a place to live. Simultaneously, we scoured the city in every direction for an apartment to rent or a house to buy. We looked for a suitable house. I decided to rent one of the Holiday Apartments to live in until the house on which I had made a down payment was built and ready for occupancy. As usual, the intent to purchase a house was based solely on my ability to afford a monthly mortgage. The Holiday Apartments at 500 East Robin Lane were on the east side of the city. In comparison, the property site on South Seventeenth Avenue was just west of the East Main Canal. Twenty-fourth Street, as it descends westward from the mesa into the Yuma Valley, was then the main artery into the section of housing that is known as Hacienda Estates.

As parents with a young child, we were very cautious in selecting our "squatter's rights." Under scrutiny was a home site where the rules of safety and decency prevailed. Subsequently, Le could develop and play in a neighborhood without interference, assaults, insults, and threats. The location of the Holiday Apartments and Hacienda Estates met the aforementioned criteria. Having secured desirable living quarters, we returned to Tucson until our final move to Yuma. This relocation occurred sometime in August of 1976. With the help of an assistant, we loaded our belongings onto a U-Haul truck. Near the midnight hour, we trekked westward through the Sonoran Desert via Interstate 10 and Interstate 8, on through Dateland, Mohawk Valley, Wellton, Telegraph Pass, The Foothills, and into Yuma. This time our destination was 550 East Robin Lane—our first residence in the city of Yuma. There, we resided for approximately four months.

Chapter 3

A Neophyte in Action

Orientation for the New Teachers

A few days later, in the month of August, I reported to Yuma High School for the newly hired teacher orientation. Administrators and department heads, relative to their subjects, led the orientation. If I recall correctly, orientation for the new teachers was held over one or two days. Following was the general assembly that included the regular teachers. At orientation, the new teachers were given lots of mind-boggling information. This information consisted of rules, regulations, policies, and various procedures on how to deal with students who posed disciplinary problems. In my view, the extensive magnitude of such information was too much to digest in a short period. It was as if I was being bombarded all over again—not with projectiles and missiles that could destroy me—but by the massive information that overloaded me. At the appropriate time, in the general faculty meeting, the department heads introduced the new teachers to their fellow staff members. The Yuma High School staff unanimously welcomed the neophytes.

While my career within the public school system was in progress, my responsibility for and accountability to Le's education was not in any manner neglected. Le had reached the age for kindergarten. For the first time, he was enrolled in the public school system in Arizona. Le's mother and I met with the principal of James B. Rolle Elementary School, the school in which Le was assigned and registered for kindergarten.

Meanwhile, I was exceedingly busy learning the in-house intricacies of the social studies department of Yuma High School. That year (1976–1977), the freshman social studies curriculum commenced with team teaching. I was assigned to team teach with Mrs. J-An Walker. With one exception, all the classes that I was assigned to teach were for freshmen. The sixth period American History class was comprised of all junior high school students. The new teacher was responsible and accountable for two preparations.

Personally, team teaching was an inappropriate strategy for instructing freshmen students. Synchronization on the part of both teachers was essential in order to implement an effective teaching method and strategy for freshmen. This plan of action was ineffective and futile among some teachers. Each teacher in a team teaching situation should maintain the professional importance of his fellow colleague. Neither should minimize the professional role of his or her teammate. Students were quick to sense any teacher's conduct that was less than professional.

A suitable building that inhibits disruption is where freshman classes should be held. In 1976–1977, the freshman classes were held in the old physical education (PE) building. It was constructed of concrete stones with no windows and a tin roof. The building was often the scene of where students had bombarded the roof with objects, such as rocks.. This rambunctious assault interfered with the students' concentration and disrupted the learning process. The large class sizes alone (sixty or more students per class) negatively impacted the students enough! Like any teacher who is concerned about the well-being of his students, I diligently tried numerous times to capture and identify the culprit(s), but to no avail.

In the midst of every Yuman's plan of action was the impact of a natural phenomenon. One morning—September 7, 1976—the students of the first-period class gathered in the door of the classroom. They were highly exhilarated at the sight and sound of heavy rain. I implored them to return to their seats, but they remained at the entrance/exit door, excited about the rain! Mrs. Walker, amused, said that the students were not accustomed to rain.

As it was, my planning period followed the completion of first period. I used this time for resource reading and for planning for other relevant classroom work. Once during the second period, Mrs. Taylor, the department secretary, came from the office to the old PE building to inform me that school had been dismissed for the remainder of the day. She further stated that the staff and students had gone home because Hurricane Kathleen was on a direct course to Yuma. When I left the PE building and went to the social studies office, I do not recall seeing anyone else on the campus other than the secretary. Knowing what damage a hurricane could cause, I called Le's school to see if I needed to pick him up. Although I had difficulty getting through on the telephone, someone in the principal's office assured me that all the children had left and arrived home safely. What a relief! Once the concern of Le's safety was confirmed, I left the campus and drove home.

Coming northward from the Gulf of California, Hurricane Kathleen rolled and rumbled through Yuma like a freight train. Her prevailing wind velocity was approximately eighty miles per hour. Anything that could not withstand her wind was toppled. The dirt, the grit, the sand, and the debris pelted anyone and everything in her way.

After the hurricane had violently thrashed Yuma, I decided to go outside to assess whether Betsy was damaged. Le came out with me. He was old enough to observe the adverse effects of the hurricane.

"Dad! Dad!" Le shouted. "That wind was bionic!" He noticed that Kathleen had toppled part of the property's concrete wall that was on the north side.

"Dad, it looks like God was trying to kill us!"

"No, son. God was not trying to kill us," I replied.

Procuring visual aids for my classes was like pulling hens' teeth. This was just another hoop through which I had to jump and slide. The reality of this new ground was a challenge. It was laden with all kinds of hidden roots and briers and brambles. Like a persistent plow, I had to cut through the new ground without breaking the plow. For example, I consulted a veteran social studies teacher concerning the availability of a thermofax machine. He emphatically stated that he had never heard of a thermofax machine, nor did he know that any such machine existed. Not for one moment did I suppose that this teacher was being truthful. What he said was just a willful act of his own chicanery. The veteran teacher did not deter me from further inquiry for a thermofax machine. Applicable in this instance was one of my father's sage expressions: "Root, hog, or die!" Later, in an adjoining room to the veteran teacher's classroom, I discovered a thermofax machine! The only thing that separated him from the thermofax machine was a closed door and a few paces into the next room.

Lost and hidden in the complex new ground was a 16-mm film projector and overhead projector. These projectors and other audio-visual equipment remained lost and hidden until I met Mr. Kelly, the director of audiovisual, at a faculty picnic. Planned and orchestrated by Mr. Biltz, an administrator, this particular picnic was held at Joe Henry Park. Faculty outings of this kind provided an opportunity for me to meet other members of staff on a personal and informal level. That contact with Mr. Kelly opened the door for scheduled audio-visual equipment on the basis of need. Later, during my time at Yuma High School, after Mr. Kelly had arrived, the department head (Mrs. Turner) asked me if she could station some audio-visual equipment in my classroom. Of course, I obliged and was honored. She needed a central place, under watchful and protective eyes, to leave some select equipment in Snider building. Now the intricate wall or system, which I had previously experienced in procuring audio-visual equipment, crumbled. For the next twenty years, audio-visual equipment was readily available for my classroom. Occasionally, there was in-house rivalry among some fellow social studies teachers because the equipment was placed in my classroom. In this matter, I knew that the Almighty was acting on my behalf to penetrate the complex maze of my need to procure equipment.

Maintaining the equipment was voluntary and important. Maintenance was always proper: cleaning and dusting, lubricating, making minor adjustments, and replacing bulbs, and correcting the lighting sensitivity. I had learned how to do this kind of maintenance at the two-year college and university levels. As I recall, no one there knew how to do this before I took it on.

As I learned the traditions and customs and mores at Yuma High, time was fleeting. The sound of students' academic performance was reverberating in the background. That meant that grades were almost due. In 1976, the school year was divided into two semesters. Each semester featured nine weeks. Grades were due every quarter, followed with a first- and a second-semester grade computation. Whatever grade I had awarded each student had to be consistent with Mrs. J-An Walker's grade computation. After all, we were involved in the new team-teacher approach. As stated earlier, our students were all in one classroom—comprised of a single class. Mrs. Walker was very helpful and willingly aided me concerning the students' grade computation.

Interestingly, the completion of the first semester of 1976–1977 school year also marked the completion of our family home. The Jacobson Company built the house in Hacienda Estates, just below what is now Yuma Regional Medical Center. Relocating from Robin Lane to South Seventeenth Avenue was a pleasant change. A hearty thanks was expressed to the following well-intentioned men who made this possible: Mr. R. Garcia of social studies, Mr. T. Turley of Title 1 Reading and Mr. Wride, Mr.

Turley's father-in-law, who was visiting from the state of Utah. Of their own volition and without any cost to me, these men volunteered their time and labor to ensure that all furniture was moved in and set up in our newly built home. In fact, Mr. Garcia provided the vehicle in which our furniture and household belongings were loaded and transported. In a genuine sense, the afore-mentioned colleagues, along with Mr. Wride, displayed their generosity toward me and my family at an opportune time. Consequently, my family and I celebrated our first Christmas ever in a newly built home.

Following the Christmas holidays, the commencement of the new year (1977) ushered in the second semester. At the start of the second semester, we also received a new teacher for the freshman social studies teaching team. Now I was faced with an entire different personality. For personal reasons, Mrs. Walker was on leave. To maintain a professional stance, I had to learn to function peacefully with the new teacher, someone I knew nothing about, "Mrs. Se." Early in the semester, it was observed that "Mrs. Se" took the liberty of not coming to the classroom on time.

In my opinion, there were several fundamental flaws in this new teacher's approach in handling freshman students. First, as any experienced educator knows, one needs to engage high school students in their daily activities as quickly as possible. Precious time allocated for meaningful learning exercises should never be compromised. Prompt attendance and professional guidance on the part of the teacher are absolutely essential. Second, "Mrs. Se" had a habit of behaving like one of the students. Social and behavioral characteristics of this kind reduced the teacher's ability to affect and influence appropriate classroom behavior. Other adverse effects were disciplinary problems on the part of some students. Third, this new teacher would often overlook disruptive and inappropriate student behavior. To ignore this type of behavior is to create a ripple effect that reproduces escalated misbehavior among some students. Eventually, disciplinary problems became rampant.

"Mrs. Se" now recognized that the height of disciplinary problems warranted special attention. Unknown to me, she then arranged with the department head to assemble her fifth-period class in another classroom. For the first time, the team-teaching approach for freshman social studies was breached! This decision and arrangement was made before the completion of the school year. Its intended purpose was to minimize student misbehavior and mischief. In that classroom, a reliable source disclosed that "Mrs. Se" was the target of flying objects hurled by mischievous students. Meanwhile, I spent the remainder of the school year teaching my fifth-period class in the old PE building. At last, there were no significant disciplinary problems.

I, too, was not insulated from challenging students. One day, a young man who was an enrollee in my American history class verbally exploded like a grenade. "Mr. Smith," he stated as he stood towering over me before leaving the classroom, "you are the biggest fool on the whole school campus."

I replied, "While you are walking out of class, go directly to the principal's office." This young man was officially taken out of my class. I do not recall whether or not he was expelled from school.

The other students were irate young ladies who were dissatisfied with the way I taught American history. These young ladies, without my permission, walked out of class and complained to the principal about how I taught. He praised me for doing a good job in the classroom. Forthrightly, he said, "Sam, we administrators can tell how well a teacher is teaching by what the students are saying." In a practical sense, the principal reproved these young students. He informed them that they should have never walked out of class. He also admonished them that I did not have to let them re-enter my class, before he advised the students to return to class and apologize for having walked out of class. It is a pleasure to report that each student followed the principal's corrective advice. That principal was the definition of teacher support, and as a disciplinarian, he quickly sensed that these students could assume responsibility and accountability for their behavior, if they were guided to think. I profoundly respected and honored this principal, Mr. Martinez.

Two colleagues with whom I worked closely emphasized their professional accomplishment of a master's degree. No other fellow colleagues spoke of their laurels. Later, I learned that one teacher was probably exaggerating. How sobering it was for a beginning teacher to hear about the accolades of educators who had advanced themselves in the field of education! Now, the sound of the aforementioned words further encouraged *this* neophyte to make a calculated decision. If I were going to remain in the field of education, it would be advantageous to earn a master's degree. Near the close of the 1976–1977 school year, I enrolled in a graduate program and began graduate studies.

The closing of the school year was somewhat militaristic in that the teacher was required to process students out as if they were soldiers who had received orders to transfer out of their current unit. The teacher was required to return all paraphernalia that was dispensed to him or her during the school year. Upon doing so, a teacher was officially processed (signed) out from that specific station. Aside from turning in all the annual assigned equipment and other items, one was also required to turn in all quarter and semester grades, permanent grade completions and absences, administrative-issued grade books, and a hands-on final exam where required. These were the year-end standardized procedures that the administration had in place during the many years that I was a public servant at Yuma High School. Moreover, the social studies department head's year-end requisite was that his teachers write a statement of their goals and objectives. Inclusive in the statement was one's specific goals and objectives—and whether one accomplished them. Upon submitting this requisition, one was officially cleared for the 1976–1977 school year.

And so it was. I knew that the Supreme One above was the one who gave me the enduring strength and the determination to complete my first year of teaching. What I did not know then was that it was just the first of twenty more years to come!

Chapter 4

Graduate School: Learning How to Learn

As has been alluded, graduate school quickly convened in the summer of 1977, after the end of the Yuma High School year. That summer, I attended both summer sessions. The classes were taught by professors who came from the University of Arizona in Tucson. Those professors who did not drive to Yuma would usually take a flight from Tucson into Yuma International Airport. Sometimes I would meet one of the professors at the airport and transport him to his accommodations or classroom. Most of the classes were held and taught on the campus of Arizona Western College, which is approximately eighteen miles east of Yuma, just north of Interstate 8. Most of us graduate students were teachers who taught in the public school system. We had the commonality of being in the field of education and working with children. My personal intent was to earn a master's degree in secondary education.

The hours spent in graduate studies, planning for the classroom and teaching, meeting with students and with parents, staying on target with administration, home front parenting, Bible-based activities, and family and marital obligations were enormous. Philosophically, I quickly learned that graduate work entailed countless hours of research upon research, writing upon writing, analysis upon analysis, synthesis upon synthesis, discussion upon discussion, and so forth. Other skills were an integral part of graduate studies and were as equally profound and important. These skills included critical thinking, problem-solving, inquisitive study, insightful apprehending, and relevant projects tailored to one's method of teaching. Individuals who made classroom presentations, as well as those who spoke for the collective group, were added resources who provided further meaningful learning styles and strategies to the curriculum.

Personally, graduate school was like being in a field that had precious and hidden treasures. In confident expectation, one had to enter the field and search for treasures in order to find them.

Those treasures that were retrieved were more precious than gold, silver, diamonds, and other precious metals or stones. I was among those who were in the field, gathering all the treasures of knowledge that could help me in my teaching career. This is mainly why I enjoyed graduate school, along with its suitable classroom pragmatism, more than I did undergraduate school. For the first time, I viewed this type of school as a means of learning how to learn.

Finally, the day came when I had completed all the bona fide courses that were preliminary to the final examination. Passing the final exam was the rite of passage to a master's degree in secondary education. Although I had some concerns about expressing myself well enough on the exam, I did prevail. It took me approximately four and a half hours to complete the exam. The university instruction emphasized that one respond with quality, not quantity With all my focus and mental capacity, I attacked the exam with my best shot. An examiner, who had a PhD background, called and congratulated me on having earned a master's degree. He further stated, "You can now tell your family that you have a master's degree." What a joy it was to hear those words.

Soon afterward, I continued in the university's graduate program. Some of the courses I pursued were those that could eventually lead to a degree in administration. Gradually, I became disenchanted because of what I observed within the public school system. Some decisions and infrastructural chicanery did not align with my moral and social conscience and character.

Sometimes my son would attend classes with me. He enjoyed the classes as much as I did, though he was the youngest person in the class. I observed that he showed a keen interest in what was going on in class and understood what was taught. To capitalize on his ability, I would sometimes let him do my assignments. To my amazement, he would get 98 to 99 percent of the assignment correct. This gave me more opportunity to do other complex assignments. Sometimes I would accompany him to the university library and place him on an assignment while I attended class. When the class dismissed, I would return to the library, where he would have completed the assignment. I must say, my son had a sharp scholarly ability.

Somewhere following the mid-1980s, my wife and I decided to take graduate courses at Trinity College in Washington, DC. We would travel from Yuma, Arizona to Washington, DC during the summer. At Trinity College, I earned thirty graduate units through several summer enrollment programs. After that, another change of venue in pursuit of graduate studies ensued. This time, my wife and I enrolled in California Polytechnic University (Cal Poly) at San Luis Obispo. In several summer classes, I earned thirty graduate units.

In the 1990s, near the beginning of the school year, I was eagerly trying to impress upon a freshmen class the importance of remaining in school and that students excel in their classes. Using myself as an example, I stated that I had gone to school for a period of twenty years. One student, who did not intend for me to hear him, said in a low-toned voice, "You surely must be dumb!"

Planning for the Classroom and Teaching

In order to man their class effectively, teachers spend countless hours perfecting the art of their subject. The art of preparation included day-to-day reading and writing, developing lesson plans, gathering resource materials, previewing visual aids, keeping abreast of current events, generating student excitement and participation in the learning process, re-assessing and evaluating what worked better in classroom instruction, and so forth. Each of these things, and many more, were my modus operandi for more than twenty years as a classroom teacher.

As one can perceive, recognize, and comprehend, a teacher's role is multifarious. Not only is the responsibility for the daily preparation of the learning environment on the teacher's shoulders, the daily care of his or her students is exceedingly important as well. As members of a microcosm of general society, students come to class with all kinds of problems, concerns, and frustrations. They often vent their frustrations on the teacher, simply because the teacher is the representative authority they see day to day, not the principal or the disciplinarian. Thus, it becomes the teacher's role to deal with all kinds of concerns, problems, and frustrations that are often bottled up in students. A teacher who is open to this myriad of issues from his students establishes the foundation of lasting sensitivity that helps students go through the educational system with a greater sense of self-worth, belonging, and caring.

In addition to being state-certified, a teacher needs to be caring, and to exude to children love, patience, and tolerance. Obviously, this kind of passionate desire must always be maintained on a professional level. In order to engage students in the purpose of learning, the teacher must have a genuine love for and an interest in them. It also reduces the levels of stress and frustration. Also, patience that is exuded toward students gives them time to re-adjust their attitude. This is a period in which the student has time to view his or her reaction and correct undesirable behavior. It further allows the student to escape to the time-out safety zone. Tolerance is exuded toward students when the teacher becomes the object of displeasure and vulnerability to the students, parents, and administrators. All three groups usually blame the teacher for the young learner's behavioral inefficiencies and misguided behavior. Sometimes, patience and tolerance are inseparable. They simply co-exist and often render the teacher as the scapegoat of the student's displeasure. If the teacher is not careful, he may very well see his job as a thankless career. Here is a case in point: One day, I spoke to one student about his misbehavior. The student replied, "Watch it! After all, you are nothing but a teacher!" I was startled at his words but powerless to do anything.

Meeting with Students and with Parents

Teachers who are involved in the daily instruction of students must offer an available period to meet with the students. The student's time to meet should, if possible, be based on an optional schedule. On a daily basis, I arrived at school from one and a half to two hours before the beginning of first period and was available to see students. In addition, students could see me during their lunch period and during my planning period. Personal meetings of this kind were most effective, because it afforded me the opportunity to provide individualized instruction and guidance that helped students succeed in their assignments. Some students need a "nudge" (as Daddy would say) in knowing how to best proceed with their assignments.

Most of the parents I was fortunate to meet were genuinely interested in their sons or daughters doing well in class. They were supportive in knowing that their youngster adhered to the classroom decorum that promoted meaningful learning experiences. Seldom did any parent make an attempt to change my philosophy on how to manage my classroom, but some did pose their own personal views on some of my educational philosophies. For example, a parent once said to me that she disagreed that I was sanctioning interracial marriage. I replied that a student once asked if I would marry an Anglo lady. "Absolutely yes," I replied. "If I was in love with a lady, and such a decision was mutually consented, I would marry her whether she was Anglo, two-toned, grisly gray, or yellow, or black."

That parent still said, "I disagree with you. People should stick to their own kind."

In another case, an after-school conference was held with the parent, the administrator, and yours truly. For approximately two and a half hours, this parent tried to persuade me to change the grade that his daughter had earned. His accusation was that I had made a mistake in his daughter's grade computation. This was a clear case of an untruth. Moreover, it was against my conscience and would show outright dishonesty to award the student a grade that she did not earn. The administrator was very supportive in my decision and said to the parent that he did not recommend changing the grade; however, the parent kept demanding that I approve his daughter's grade change. Finally, I gave the parent my grade book in the presence of the principal and said, "You change it and sign whatever you need to sign. I will have nothing else to do with this."

Staying on Target with Administration

Chaperoning was a sure assignment for beginning teachers. The chaperone duties to which I am referring took place during evening-school events that were held near the beginning of the school year. Like a loyal soldier, we beginning teachers and other assigned teachers reported to the administration and those in charge. We were all there to assist the administrators and to help ensure a safe campus. This provided another means for the new teacher to learn the layout of the school campus. Moreover, I intently observed every nook and cranny where students should not be. With the exception of an entire school campus assembly, we beginning teachers were exposed to a greater number of students than those assigned to our classes.

On a daily basis, I never knew what I would face from the administration. Seldom was I summoned to an administrator for something that was on a positive note. Most of the meetings centered around expressions or sayings that were taken out of context. I made many trips to the administrative office and to its brainchild (the counseling department). In either place, I often heard the cracking sound of a whip with disparaging news. Parents were sometimes supercharged with anger because of what their youngster reported about me.

I vividly recall two incidents.

Normally, I did not participate in any Halloween events. For this particular Halloween, I relented and purchased candy to dispense to the students who sported a Halloween costume. Any student who acknowledged that his or her costume was Halloween-ware received candy. There was one young lady who sported what appeared to be a camouflaged military uniform. I asked her twice if her attire was for Halloween. Each time she answered no. So I did not give her any candy. Shortly afterward, I was summoned to the administration office. The principal reported that the student's father called him and said that I had made fun of and laughed at what his daughter was wearing. I informed the principal of the aforementioned and further said that what the student said to her father was not true. Hence, what I had intended to be a goodwill gesture on Halloween was discontinued on the day of its origin.

In another incident, the counseling office arranged an appointment for me to meet with the parents of one of my students. Their youngster had personified me to his father as a tyrant and a vicious man.

At the very onset of the meeting, the young man's father said, "You are not mean. You do not even present yourself as a mean person."

The student's mother kept repeating, "I told you so," as she replied to her husband. "It is our son who has the problem, not Mr. Smith."

The father went on to say that his son had personified me as a big black man who was bad and mean, and who had also broken a stick into pieces when he hit one of his students. Of course, after I established a common ground with the student's parents, we all departed on a cheerful note. Before our departure, the father pledged his assurance that he would work on his son's attitude. Ironically, I never observed a need for attitude adjustment. The son did not display a blatantly resentful persona.

Home Front Parenting

Interestingly, children are the world's greatest investment within their family, state, and nation at large. Consequently, parents should be devoted to their well-being and training with all deliberate speed. This is why as a parent, I am committed to the aforementioned practice in the rearing of my own son. As one can clearly perceive, parenting and training children are interlaced with several qualified cohesions or coefficients. Exuded in a child's training and rearing, these parental cohesions or coefficients heartily should assist the children in learning accountability and responsibility, security and tranquility, stability and protection, caring and nurturing, intimacy and benevolence, flexibility and gentleness, and so forth. This further implies that parents can exhibit those social and moral standards on a level their children can emulate.

Spending time with a child is another important way of developing a lasting relationship and strong bond between parents and their children. Perhaps Daddy said it best, as he was relating to me what his advice was to a certain individual. He said that he advised the individual to come and get his children and that he should spend time with his children. Daddy went on to say, "I took up time with you boys." He indeed did. Daddy was a family man who spent tireless hours with his children and a father who took his children many places. Likewise, I intentionally spent memorable times with my son. I took him to various amusement attractions, field trips, educational tours, and historic sites. For example, we were either touring or had recently completed a field trip of Ford Motor Company in Mahwah, New Jersey when he said, "Dad, I will be the only one in the whole school who has been on a field trip at the Ford Motor Plant." His saying was probably accurate, since he was attending Rancho Viejo Elementary School in Yuma, Arizona.

Now, communication is as equally important as spending quality time with a child. Parents are obligated to talk to their children, to listen to their children, to guide their children, to correct their children, and to let their children express themselves. Parents who build this kind of relationship with their children often lay the foundation on which they can learn the inner character of their own children. They can further observe the underlined intent of their child's thinking and behavior. If my son's mind would openly lean toward that which was reprehensible, I would say, "Son, you do not need to do that. There are enough deviant people in our community and society. You do not need to become one of them." In the best interest in their children's well-being and the integrity of the local, national, and global community, parents need to redirect their child's thinking and behavior when it is necessary. Parental guidance and influence often have an impressionable imprint on the minds and the hearts of the youth, as they are surely the decision-makers and the leaders of both present-day and future generations.

Bible-based Activities

Shortly after I relocated to Yuma, I received

a hand-delivered letter from a Second Baptist Church mother. One of my students was the courier of Mother R. Shine's letter. The hand-delivered letter came with a special message from Miss T. Shaw, who boldly said: "[Mother Shine] wants you to get in touch with her!" Having learned that I was an ordained minister, Mother Shine asked if I would minister at Second Baptist on the Sunday that their pastor would not be there. The pastor at that time only ministered every other Sunday. To make sure that I did not usurp the pastor and church officials' authority, I met with them. Everyone was pleased that I agreed to minister on those Sundays.

In his disclosure, Rev. R. Reed said to me that he was not interested in returning to Yuma and pastoring Second Baptist. He further stated that he had accepted every other Sunday because there were those members who had beseeched him to come and pastor. Aside from this, Rev. R. Reed said that he already had a pastorate in Phoenix, Arizona, with which he was well pleased.

When I started proclaiming God's Word at Second Baptist Church, attendance was small. In time, church attendance improved tremendously, and quite a few people became regular attendees. Then, approximately seven months later, the head deacon informed me that I would no longer be needed. He further explained that the pastor would be returning to Yuma the next Sunday to attend to his flock on a full-time basis. What the deacon said was surely a far cry from what Pastor Reed had said earlier. Really, what unfolded before my presence was the subtle art of deceit and deception. From that time onward, I became an itinerant preacher who proclaimed the Word of God throughout various towns and cities.

Family and Marital Obligations

As I grew up in rural southeastern North Carolina, I observed Daddy as a man who sold himself to the support of his family. Seeing that the work ethic was an integral part of my life, it continued even after I married in my early twenties. Countless hours were invested in the economic support of the nuclear family. Experiences had already taught me that menial jobs could not measure up to the lifestyle that I desired and that I wanted for my family. So I pursued higher education with all deliberate speed. Each level of accomplishment I considered as a family accomplishment—at least from the standpoint of my opinion. The end result was the enablement of a much better life for my family.

What I am revealing now has nothing to do

with the lady to whom I am presently married. During the period of the 1960s to the mid-1980s, we did not even know each other. I am prefacing this out of respect for my wife and so that the reader can remain focused on the family structure with which I was formally involved. It appeared that all was well within my household in those days, but there was turbulence within my marriage that was greater than the mighty force of a tornado. Yet I was oblivious to it.

As it was, in the early 1980s, my wife left her family under the guise of attending the University of Arizona. According to her, she enrolled in enough classes to potentially earn eighteen credits per semester. Within the same semester, she gradually dropped course after course. Consequently, some semesters, she did not earn any credits. To this day, I know nothing about that lady ever earning a degree from the University of Arizona.

Shortly after she had moved to Tucson, a neighbor approached me and said that he had heard that my wife was going to divorce me. In response, I stated that I did not know anything about a divorce. He further said that the one involved often was the last to learn about such news. Sometime later in Tucson, my wife voiced that she wanted a legal separation. I rejected this notion and said no. I said that, if anything, there would be a divorce. That was the first time that I had ever heard of a legal separation.

The day of infamy came when I decided to go to Tucson unannounced. I procured a key to my wife's apartment and entered. There I found striking evidence that openly violated the sanctity of the marriage. That kind of violation, unlawfulness, and disunity drove a sharp stake into our marriage. The stake then impaled the heart of the marriage—thus causing the death of the marriage. "It died until it could not die anymore," as the saying goes. Thus, a divorce was granted in mid-1985.

Chapter 5

The Ugly Head of Racism

The ugly head of racism should not have any place of existence within the public arena, especially on the site of a public educational institution or any place of learning. Little did I know that I would hear the reverberating sound of the "N-word" ("nigger") for approximately eight years on the campus of Yuma High School. The N-word was repugnant and denigrating. I hated the sound of that word but could never identify the student(s) who shouted it. Calling someone the N-word was, and still is, insulting to one's humanity and has no place in the public or private domain. Unfortunately, that racist word echoed one to two years before I officially retired from Yuma High School.

I once entered the classroom of one of my colleagues for a personal business. There was a European male student who shouted in my face—eyeball to eyeball—"Nigger!" That made me angry, and I released a flood of choice words to that student. With the cooperation of that student's teacher, he was ordered to report to my classroom and issue a personal apology. I gladly accepted the student's apology. But I then I wondered, as I do now, whether the student meant it from his heart or entered the escape route of passing his course through the process of an apology.

Other contemptuous episodes were shockingly disdainful and apparent. One was the exposure (or "flashing") of the rear of one's personal anatomy. This student would occasionally open my door, quickly disrespect me, and then run down the hall as fast as lightning. Of course, the majority of the students in the class would find such behavior amusing. The other incident occurred during a student assembly in Snider Auditorium. Someone on the second-floor level above spat on me! What an insult and dishonor and spiteful thing that someone would do to another individual. Truthfully speaking, that is a gross violation of one's dignity!

Aside from a minute number of students, let us view the blatant effects of racism that several colleagues directed toward me. These educators were not even as sophisticated as most of the students; they always had an audience to express their stereotypical racist putdowns. The first incident involved a well-seasoned educator, whom I greeted shortly after I entered onto the campus. He repeatedly harassed me with the following words, "Hey, boy. Where are you going?" I hated the sound of those words. As a neophyte to the system, I was shocked by what he said, and I did not know how to respond. This daily insult bothered me immensely, such that I would have rather walked a mile to avoid seeing him! This racist expression continued until I quipped one day, "What are you? The Great White Father?"

Facing the triangle, I was standing with a group of teachers underneath the breezeway at Yuma High School. There we were discussing various graduate courses in which one could enroll. Among those selections was one on effective communication. One of the teachers suddenly belched, "Mr. Smith, that would be a good course for you to take, because you do not know how to communicate."

I replied, "I do not have any problem communicating. I know how to talk." Needless to say, his paternalistic view was not acceptable.

I encountered another racist colleague as I was standing in line with a number of teachers, who kept constantly repeating, "Sambo!" Finally, I had heard enough. I turned to him in disgust and said, "Are you a racist?" Calling me Sambo was despicable and offensive. He epitomized Stanley Elkins's Sambo personality. According to Elkins, slaves in the colonies (and later in the United States) were relegated to the Sambo personality. Black American slaves were docile, silly, lazy, shiftless, and had to be told what to do. To some extent, as Elkins noted, that personality character transcended to Black American descendants and to their children's children in twentieth-century society. Briefly put, in the minds of some individuals, Black Americans and other ethnic minorities never escaped the imposition of the racist caste system to which they were assigned.

Interestingly, one would surmise that the principals at Yuma High were not aware of the racist acts that were directed toward me. There were other "racist hawks" on campus who overtly expressed racist overtones; however, their subtle acts of racism were not significant enough to report.

Chapter 6

An Educator's Perspective on Education

In a highly technological society and within the global community, education is essential. It is the spring well that raises the fountain of hope and opportunity that enlightens a society and the global community. Individuals who drink deep from the fountain of knowledge are the ones whose abilities and capabilities enrich a nation of people and the international society. A nation that sanctions public education for its citizenry makes for a better international connection and a better cultural exchange of ideas and languages and international trade and economic relations. Now, the pragmatist of this ideology had its origin in the social structure of any given society.

One practical implementation of my philosophy involved my creation of a syllabus. Each semester, my approach was to help the students become acquainted with the social studies syllabus and to have a practical knowledge of its usage. Although it was not a district or a social studies departmental requirement, the idea of a social studies syllabus was first disseminated to me through Mr. R. Drysdale, the social studies department head. Because it was tailored to the needs of each grade level, the syllabus, I felt, was a masterful creation that I implemented my second year at Yuma High School. I incorporated it in my plans until my retirement in 1997.

Designed to foster relevant learning experiences, the syllabus featured several categories such as evaluation feedback, classroom behavior and attitude, attendance and tardies, mini-research papers, outside activities (seven or more assignment choices), resource speakers/persons, the student record, and so forth. After a thorough explanation had been given on the detailed usage of the syllabus, each student was required to develop an individual contract, and he had to present a copy to the instructor. The student was required to maintain his copy in his notebook, while the instructor retained a copy in his file. For each contracted assignment, the student had to decide on the grade that he would earn per quarter or six weeks. In addition, the student approximated the points (based on academic and classroom performance) that he planned to earn on each contracted assignment project of his own choosing. I would always encourage and counsel students to choose those assignments or projects that best suited their interest, and to record the points earned on the student record sheet. Consequently, one could maintain an accurate accounting of his current grade point average.

With the exception of the evaluation feedbacks, each student was greatly involved in the decision making of his academic performance. Many students were very successful in their choices of the learning experiences. Classroom behavior, attitude, attendance, and tardies were bonuses in the multiplicity of alternative assignments from which they could choose. As a result, numerous alternative assignments were displayed upon the walls, on tables, and the floor and the ceiling of my classroom. Some were in my file cabinet. They too were made available to the students. Among the alternative assignments were picturesque projects, colorful collages, artistic creations, creative writings, ingenious sayings, inventive portraits, resourceful studies, cultural depictions, and so forth. Moreover, many students' critical reviews and self-chronologies were made available as learning examples to their peers.

Lectures and discussions were an integral part of the classroom instruction. As it was, the social structure was the basis of most lectured discussions. There, I would explain to the students that the social structure was, and still is, the foundation of any given society. Designated by a definite boundary, within a society there are eight basic institutions: family, education, economics, government (politics), religion, recreation (entertainment), health, and the military. These institutions, as I pointed out, form the framework that builds a nation. They are the systematic channels through which culture, languages, customs, traditions, mores, and values are learned, shared, and exchanged by the citizenry. Furthermore, permeating and pervading every portion of a society, culture and languages and traditions and mores and values and subcultures ensure the viability of a people and its nation at large.

Though all students were required to take notes, they were encouraged to participate in the discussion and to ask questions that were germane to the topic. It was astonishing what some quick-witted students would contribute. As I recall, there was a day when I was discussing the extended family and the nuclear family. I pointed out that their grandparents were the origin of their parents. As usual, when their parents reached the age of their majority, they met, fell in love, and got married. This final stage, I said, is called matrimony.

Some young lady said, "And later, babymony?" Of course, there was laughter.

Then another young lady followed, "And after that, alimony."

Obviously these young ladies understood and knew the reality of the topic and what could happen in one's life. Students delighted in exercising their creativity.

At his request, one young man obtained permission to mimic me. This memorable event usually took place near the closing of the semester, and happened only occasionally. Some students were just exceedingly skillful in the performing arts. They could mimic me to the very persona of my being. I would sit in the rear of my classroom and watch intently. The student's playacting scene, from beginning to end, impersonated my mannerisms, gestures, demeanor, stance, movement, speech, sound, tone, and action. Interestingly, the student's ability to impersonate his teacher was of superior quality. I was imbued with laughter to the point of tears! In addition, this student's peers were full of joy and laughter.

It was as if the whole audience had been administered laughing gas!

Personally, I believe an ideal school is one in which most classes are held from 7 AM to 12 noon each day. Inherent in this proposal are some exceptions, which we will later discuss. The core curricula of classes would meet from one and a half to two hours daily. Our classes would consist of two divisions: required and elective or alternative classes. Required and elective classes would be available for those students whose academic interests and abilities would prepare them for college or university studies that emphasized an academic background experience. Students who decide to study the subjects of their own choice are more likely to increase their learning retention and attention span on any given subject.

Alternative classes would be made available for those students whose interests were in the applied technical field or in the arts. Encompassed in the applied technical field or arts is specified training for each student—even while one is enrolled in his field of study. In each field of study, the student's training would be under the supervision of various participating businesses within the community. For clarity, here are several subjects that meet the criterion of the applied technical field or of the arts: automotive mechanics, automotive body repair, culinary art, beauty stylist (barber and beautician), decorative florist, and so forth.

Scheduled classes for the applied technical studies would meet daily from 7:00 AM to 12 noon, as mentioned earlier. These students would remain in the same classroom for the school day. All their other subjects—English, mathematics, social science, etc.—would be taught in the same classroom. The students' curriculum would be a combination of classroom instruction and practical experience in their assigned business or trade. These students' practical training would continue from their freshman year to their senior year. Where possible, in cooperation with the state's certification department, the students could take the state examination or licensing certification in their trade. In that way, upon graduating from high school, one would be qualified to enter the workplace (or field) of his or her trade.

In the proposed ideal, school lunch and concession stands and athletic activities would be held after noon. A thirty-minute lunch period, along with concession, would begin at 12:05 PM. All athletic activities would convene after lunch until 3:00 PM. The athletic curriculum would include all students—both the academic and the applied technical students. In this curriculum, a multiple of physical health activities and games would be made available to the students. On the day of interscholastic games, all students would be required to attend the games without any personal cost. Aside from this, some exceptions may be applicable. For example, those students who were not interested in attending the games would be required to attend their choice of a work-study course.

Other than special circumstances, there would be no valid reason for students to remain on campus once they have completed their daily classes. Therefore, all students who completed their daily classes before school officially dismissed would be required to vacate the campus.

Chapter 7

A Father's Son

As with most children, Le increased in social and personal development and years. Le was an energetic child who was courageous and brilliant. He displayed excellence in his ability to learn, to ponder, to delve, to observe, to comprehend, to analyze, and to solve problems. When he had completed the second grade at Rancho Viejo Elementary School, Le boarded an American Airlines plane on which he flew from Sky Harbor international Airport in Phoenix to John F. Kennedy International Airport in Long Island, New York. What impressed me the most was that once he had said goodbye, he moved forward through the connected corridors on to the plane like a brave soldier whose focus was to accomplish his assigned objective.

The moment of rendezvous came when he arrived safely at John F. Kennedy Airport, where his paternal aunt and uncle openly welcomed him. His first time traveling alone in the Northeast (Wappinger Falls, Newburgh, and Middletown, New York) afforded Le the opportunity and the privilege to see many of his extended relatives. He spent a significant amount of time with both his paternal and maternal grandparents and with relatives and cousins.

Later in the summer, I traveled via Trailways from Yuma to New York City, specifically to Manhattan. After I arrived at the Port Authority (the most complex transportation center that I have ever experienced), I made my connection with the Short Line Bus System in order to travel on to Newburgh, New York. This was the first time that I had returned to Newburgh since moving away five years earlier. There, in the home of his paternal grandparents, Le and I joyfully reunited. Together, we continued enjoying our visits with his grandparents and other extended relatives until mid-August 1979.

Then in mid-August, Le's paternal grandfather Samuel Smith, Sr., maternal grandmother Cherry Gayle Williams, and I decided to attend the Smith Family Annual Reunion in rural eastern North Carolina. Before leaving the Northeast, Le's grandmother Williams and I agreed to share expenses with his grandfather Smith to the Southeast, since he was the one who provided the vehicle and transportation.

At the reunion, Le met and played with a number of relatives he had just met for the first time. Also, it was his grandmother Williams' first time attending the event. As it was, I had not attended the reunion since I was a teenager. Time had impacted my physical appearance. Aunt Lucile said, "June, you finally became a man."

"Aunt Lucile," I replied, "how old does one have to be before he becomes a man?"

She responded, "What I mean by that is that you were always so tiny."

The Smith Family Reunion ended on a positive note with blessings and well wishes that were spoken in our lives. Afterward, Le and I returned to Yuma via Trailways. His grandmother Williams accompanied us.

Two years later, Le asked that I allow him to return to Newburgh, New York, to spend more time with his paternal grandparents and other relatives. When I saw that he had confidence to make the necessary connections and travel alone to the Northeast, I decided to allow him to visit. First, I had to contact Mother and Daddy to see whether they would permit me to entrust Le to their keeping for a part of the summer. They gladly accepted. I assured them that I would come for Le upon completing a graduate course during the first summer session. Having made the arrangements for Le's reception, I went to the Trailways Bus Company and purchased Le's ticket to Newburgh. Concerning a child riding the transit alone, management's position was that the child must be able to render and care for his personal needs. An analysis of Le's schedule disclosed the time and the date and the day of his departure from Tucson, and the time and day of his arrival at the Short Line Bus Station in Newburgh. Of course, Le's grandparents were notified of the time of departure and arrival. As planned, his grandfather Smith was at the bus station, awaiting Le's arrival.

Having imparted to him all the fatherly counsel that I knew about traveling, I was there as he boarded the bus with tenacity. This young man, who was nine years and approximately eight months in age, had the "can-do" spirit of a mighty champion. I watched and waved until I could no longer see the bus.

I did not hear from Le until he had arrived at the Port Authority in New York City. A lady in The Port Authority called and asked, "Do you have a son named Le?"

"Yes," I replied. How is he doing?"

"He is fine!" she exclaimed.

"Is there any problem?" I asked.

"No," said the lady.

I went on to say that Le was on his way to visit his grandparents, who lived in New York. He was already in place to make the appropriate transfer to Newburgh.

The lady said, "We will make sure he gets on the right bus."

"Sometimes," said the lady, "children run away from home. Here in the Port Authority, we stop them."

Enduring stamina was another distinguishing feature of Le's childhood and adolescent development. He was athletically inclined and had a propensity for sports. Along with the other children in the neighborhood, Le enjoyed playing a variety of games. With their respective teams, these children often competed against one another without any adult supervision. Among themselves, they learned the strategies and the dynamics concerning the rules of fair play. As he advanced in years, Le went on to play organized sports, under the guidance of coaches. He played football, baseball, soccer, and golf, just to name a few.

As a protective father, I really did not want Le

to play football. In fact, I made a concerted effort to discourage him. From my viewpoint, the very game of football was a violent and brutal sport. The risk of permanent injuries was all too real. Before I would grant Le permission to play, I presented to him various individuals who were current victims of football injuries. He listened attentively, without any response to what I said.

I then asked, "Do you still want to play football?"

"Yes," said Le.

So I signed the papers, which granted him parental permission.

One afternoon when Le returned home from school, he said, "Dad, the coach said that I am too small to play football."

When I heard this, I was glad! I considered that news a permanent solution concerning any possible football injuries that Le may have sustained. Moreover, in my mind, the coach's decision was the final one needed so that Le would not be playing football. But his desire to play football superseded the coach's decision and my notion as well. Soon afterward, Le asked if he could play football on the Pop Warner Team. As a parent, how could I have said no?

"Yes," I replied. Here I was, seeing my son, a young lad, affirming the epitome of stamina.

Through his persistence, he found a way to play football—and without any injuries.

Interestingly, this same persistence resulted in Le's involvement in several school-related activities and awards. Serving with distinction, he was an active member of the Distributive Education Clubs of America (DECA); the National Society of the Sons of the American Revolution; the National Honor Society of Secondary Schools; the American Legion Boys State; the Arizona Athletic Trainer Association; and the Presidential Academic Witness Awards Program. In retrospect, Le's involvement in the aforementioned societies was indeed an impressive one.

In like manner, he was driven to work outside of school functions as well. Where Le asked me if he could work, I gave him permission on the condition that he maintain excellent grades. I pointed out to Le: You will have plenty of time to work, and will spend forty years or more in the workplace. You will need to work in order to gain experience in the workplace. Now is the time for you to fully concentrate on your studies and earn grades of honorable standing.

In 1987, Le had recently completed his sophomore year. Betsy (my vintage car) was the chosen vehicle for Le and me to run an errand. As we were cruising in Betsy, I asked him what he was planning to do. I continued, saying, "You do not have long. You only have eighteen months and you will have finished high school. That is not that far away."

In response, Le presented three plans of his intent to pursue higher education. He said, "Dad, my first choice is to attend West Point Military Academy. My second choice is to attend the University of Southern California (USC). My third choice is to attend the University of Arizona (U of A), your alma mater, Dad."

It pleased me that Le had heeded my counsel over the years and that his decision was to enroll in higher education.

I said to him, "If you want to attend West Point Military Academy, you can. Now, I want you to start preparing your paperwork."

Added to Le's list of daily activities was his order of paperwork and the organization of a résumé that he presented to United States Representative Morris "Mo" Udall and United States Senator John McCain. Prior to finishing high school at Yuma High, Le was nominated by Senator John McCain and received his appointment to attend West Point Military Academy. Surely, this was a milestone in the life and times of my beloved son.

Le's nomination and appointment to the

academy was in alignment with my expectations. It was the Spirit of God who revealed to me well before I learned of the exciting news that Le would attend the academy. My wife can attest to this. When I said to her that Le would attend the academy, she asked, "How do you know?"

I responded, "The Spirit of God put it in my spirit that he would."

Sometime during the last semester of Le's senior year, Senator McCain invited all appointees and their parents to his office in Phoenix. The few appointees who met had a delectable repast and got an opportunity to both converse with the senator and to hear his congratulatory address. Following his graduation, Le received a reporting date to the academy sometime in June. My wife expressed that we should take Le to West Point on his reporting date. This suggestion was well taken, and I agreed wholeheartedly. We arrived at West Point Military Academy and heard the reception address, along with Le, his fellow plebes, and their parents. Just prior to departing, I spoke some last words to Le. "Son," I said, "the ball is now in your court. It is up to you what you will do with it."

The ingenuity of Le's skills worked in his favor. He did well in his studies and graduated from West Point Military Academy four years later, on May 29, 1993.

Chapter 8

The Hatchet Era

Initially when I came to Yuma to work within the public school system, I did not come with the intent of staying. In fact, I made the following statement as I was in the actual process of relocating to Yuma: "I will complete this 1976–1977 Yuma Union District #70 school contract, and if I do not like Yuma or the working conditions, I will relocate elsewhere to teach." How little did I comprehend that in sixteen years, I would still be teaching at Yuma High School and challenging students to excel in various learning skills.

Now, the standard practice of measuring a teacher's performance was based on the teacher evaluation instrument that was administered by the administration. Overall, this was administered with a degree of fairness and honesty. For more than eighteen years, I was basically satisfied with the results, though they were less than perfect. What I never envisioned was that within the nineteenth or twentieth year of my teaching career, the "prominent assassins" would launch an agonizing and humiliating blow against my teaching style. They validated their dastardly decision through the use of teacher evaluation. In retrospect, it is appropriate to identify the four prominent assassins: "The Mailman," "The Troubleshooter," "The Linefellow," and "The Machine."

Before the "assassins" unleashed a barrage of accusatory potshots upon me, a classified employee (who was under another authoritative power base), expressed that that power base was devising fault-finding ways to axe some classified employees, who were classroom support personnel at Yuma High. This individual further stated that once the legitimate power base had finished axing the classified support personnel, this power base would go after the classroom teachers. At that time, I did not consider what the individual noted to be a weighty matter, but that was exactly what happened. Some of the classified support personnel discontinued their employment at Yuma High—either by choice or administrative request. Hence, a few years later, under the reign of "the assassins," accusatory potshots were projected upon me and other veteran teachers.

The school year commenced on a positive note. Unsuspectingly, that was what I had perceived. Later, during the first semester, I observed that "The Troubleshooter" made several unannounced entrances into my classroom. I considered this to be an excellent professional gesture because it allowed "The Troubleshooter" greater exposure to the students. The awakening moment came when "The Mailman" conveyed several inconsequential messages that emanated from "The Troubleshooter."

Standing in the entranceway of my classroom, "The Mailman" said that "The Troubleshooter" stated that when he came to my room, I was in the bathroom.

I replied, "Are you going to tell me that I cannot go to the men's room?" (Can anyone imagine that a mid-fifty-year-old individual would not be allowed to address himself in the men's room?)

Then, my classroom was the site of a message from "The Mailman." He stated that "The Troubleshooter" was in my room, and there were male students who were wearing caps. My response was that I never noticed anyone wearing his cap. If there were students wearing caps, I was sincerely unaware of it.

Perhaps this was because I had never had a problem with male children wearing caps or hats. This was what I experienced growing up as a small child in rural eastern North Carolina. In attendance at the church service were women of the sisterhood who wore wide-brim hats larger than the circle of the globe. As a small child and an individual who is still to this day short in stature, I could not see the preacher. Those wide-brim hats blocked my vision! Even then, if an innocent young male was caught with his hat on his head, some individuals would have a verbal convulsion! In comparison, I do not know what "The Troubleshooter's" problem was. I dare not think that it presented him a social problem.

One unannounced visit in my classroom was in this manner: "The Mailman" said that "The Troubleshooter" said that he came to my class-room, and that I was sitting back having a full-course meal! Nothing could have been further from the truth. I replied to both "The Mailman" and "The Troubleshooter" later that I was under a doctor's care and was taking prescribed medica-tion. When one takes certain medications, it is to be ingested with food—especially with the med-ication that I was ingesting. Also, I said to "The Troubleshooter" that if he lived long enough, his day would come when he, too, would have to take medication.

If one gets sick enough, not only will he ingest his prescription medications, but he will eat, suck, rub and smell his medication, too!

Since the early 1990s, I have been afflicted with a terrible disease due to Agent Orange exposure. On a daily basis, horrible pains jut from the top of my head. Severe knife-like pains and splitting headaches radiated throughout my skull and face. These pains were actually debilitating and affected my whole system, both internally and externally. None of this was ever disclosed to the district personnel or to any school administrator.

There was a day when "The Mailman" rushed into my class like an angry gangster, bellowing expressions that were as explosive as grenades. I do not recall why he was very upset with me, but his outburst and furious attitude toward me were as sharp as a double-edged sword. The infuriated "Mailman" and I expressed some heated words to each other. After he left the classroom, I noticed that some of the male students did not like what "The Mailman" did or said.

They said to me, "Mr. Smith, we will get him."

I replied, "No! Let him alone. It is not worth it."

The demeanor and rudeness of this person showed everything but professionalism.

One day, I received a summons that ordered me to appear before "The Linefellow" after school. I really did not know what to expect when I entered his office. To my surprise, three of the assassins were present: "The Mailman," "The Machine," and "The Linefellow." All three made a concerted attempt to pen me as the scapegoat who failed to use the freshman textbook in my classes. I told them that I had no knowledge that the textbooks had arrived and that the other freshman teachers were using them. Usually, as in previous years, the teachers were notified and the textbooks were delivered to their classrooms. "The Machine" stated that she notified each teacher and had put the notification in each mailbox. I told her that I picked up my mail every day and did not receive the notification. I then asked "The Machine" for a copy of the bulletin in question. She promised to forward a copy to me—but never did.

"The Linefellow" asked "The Mailman" who procured the mail for the social studies department.

He replied, "The secretary. But she does not procure Sam's mail."

"The Linefellow" continued, "From now on, the secretary will procure all the social studies teachers' mail. Then Sam can get his mail from the social studies department."

At least "The Linefellow" included me in the pickup mail service for the social studies department!

The worst barrages of accusatory potshots that were exerted upon me occurred when "The Troubleshooter" did his evaluation of my teaching performance. For the first time in twenty years of my teaching career, "The Troubleshooter" designated my teaching performance as unsatisfactory. Based on his prior reproachable intent toward me, undoubtedly "The Troubleshooter" now designed his insidious and reprehensible opinion toward my teaching performance. In a post-conference, I implied to him that his assessment of my teaching performance was ludicrous! I vehemently disagreed with every specific item that "The Troubleshooter" marked unsatisfactory, and refused to sign the evaluation. In addition, I wrote a formal rebuttal that refuted each of the items that was marked unsatisfactory.

Then I remembered what a classified employee had earlier articulated. She stated that the power base would axe the classroom teachers, just as it did certain classified support personnel. Unfolding before me was the classified employee's prediction. Clearly, I knew then that the assassins were prowling for the "guerilla kill." Including me, they were targeting veteran teachers to axe. I observed that these veteran teachers had been teaching for fifteen years or more. Now their careers were being stained and discredited through the use of an unsatisfactory teacher-evaluating instrument. Based on what I saw, most of these teachers were like skilled artisans. They were continually honing their professional skills in order to be more effective teachers, striving to exceed far beyond any evaluating instrument. In the hands of an assassin, fifteen to twenty years of professional upgrading and classroom experience did not matter.

What a loss of diverse talents and abilities! Some classroom teachers discontinued the practice of their profession at Yuma High because of the adverse action of the "assassins." But I took a steadfast stance. The spirit of resistance immediately entered my soul, and with the pen I previously etched opposition against the "assassins'" insidious actions. As was alluded to earlier, regretfully, there were other veteran colleagues who were targeted. I mentioned to one of them that we needed to unify and present what was happening to the Arizona Education Association representative. She responded that she did not even want the local representative to know that she had talked to me! Now I knew that the teachers were not unified. Still, there were faculty members who knew that the "assassins" had targeted certain veteran teachers to axe and discredit their professional career. They were like frightened animals that stood upon the plains, while the "assassins" viciously hacked and chopped their fellow teachers' careers with the "guerilla kill." A fellow faculty member said to me, "You do not have to take this." He suggested that I go elsewhere, but there was no other place that I wanted to teach. Rather than run like a frightened dog with his tail between his legs, I realized that I had to position myself with enough fortified strength to stand against the "assassins."

In an effort to mitigate what was happening, I met with the associate representative. I disclosed to him my intent. He suggested that I delay some of my intended actions until he could contact "Linefellow." In his advisement, the representative stated that he would recommend that my annual evaluation be conducted by a different evaluator. I pointed out that I did not trust anyone whose eminence was professional assassinations and open season for veteran teachers. Meanwhile, there were other directives upon which he asked me to act: continue teaching with excellence, write a rebuttal on the current twentieth-year teacher evaluation, and sign the evaluation in order to avoid insubordination.

Unlike all the other years, the twentieth year of my teaching career ended on an unsavory note. In spite of the numerous "potshots" that were fired upon me, I was left unscathed and still standing. On the other hand, the guerilla strategies of the "assassins" to disrupt and to annihilate my professional performance did adversely affect me. Of course, the personal strength, the time and the fight placed an undue burden and much stress upon me, thus causing me to be battle-worn and weary and fatigued. Another lesson learned was that the powers that be do not always exist in the interest of the staff—even when the faculty member's performance meets or exceeds the established standards and is impeccable. During this troublesome period, I took refuge and solace in the words of the psalmist, who stated:

> 1 If it had not been the Lord who was on our side—now may Israel say—2 If it had not been the Lord who was on our side when men rose up against us, 3 Then they would have quickly swallowed us up alive when their wrath was kindled against us; 4 Then the waters would have overwhelmed us *and* swept

us away, the torrent would have gone over us. 6 Blessed be the Lord, who has not given us as prey to their teeth! 7 We are like a bird escaped from the snare of the fowlers; the snare is broken, and we have escape! 8 Our help is in the name of the Lord who made heaven and earth. (Psalms 124:1–8, *The Amplified Bible*).

Chapter 9

Enough

There were several defining moments that best describe how my career as a public school teacher was near the end. Physical maladies and emotional fatigue and teacher burnout gripped me like an anaconda that squeezes the life out of its prey. As stated earlier, I was suffering from illnesses that resulted from Agent Orange exposure. I would arise early in the morning and sit on the edge of the bed morning upon morning before grooming for work. Many mornings, I hated to go to work, especially where I would be enclosed in a four-sided room with students! On my way to school, horrific headaches would start, only to worsen when I entered the building. Once inside the building, my digestive system became ill-affected, and I would speedily rush to the men's room. In addition, the odor within the buildings was extremely unpleasant and nauseating.

The students whom I greeted in the 1996–1997 school year were quite different from my previous classes. All of them had failed social studies, except perhaps one of the regular students! "The assassins" had struck again. They only scheduled me to teach and instruct four or five classes of the assigned students. Then I discovered that these repeaters had no interest in school and had very low self-esteem. One was that these assigned students often exuded incorrigible and clandestine classroom behavior. Collectively, their inappropriate behavior kindled each other, and soon there would be a chain of excitement like a wildfire in the classroom! These students were difficult to manage and teach. Some of them aggravated me to the point that I would find myself saying what I should have not said. For example, I said to one young man that I hoped that he would not return to class.

He replied, "I am going to tell my counselor."

"Go tell your counselor," I responded.

Whether or not the following was said to *that* young man, I would often say that I too would tell the counselor. Of course, the next day the same students would return to class.

Another time, I said to one male student, "Why are you coming to school?"

He said, "Mr. Smith, I have got to come to school! If I do not, my mama will beat me!"

I replied, "Take the beating. Your mother will stop before she kills you. Besides, a whipping only lasts no longer than ten to fifteen minutes. Then you are free until you violate your mother's rule again."

It was obvious that the students never followed these pretentious sayings. Yes, such students would return to class the next day.

The other attitude was that most of these assigned students simply were not interested in social studies and did not trust their own learning ability or capability. These students seemed to have had an aversion to world history/ geography. Grouped together, they were interdependent upon one another. In this case, not even grouping seemed to have increased their learning retention! Due to their lack of interest in the subject and their constant underhanded disruptions, the assigned students were masters at compromising effective classroom instruction. Consequently, emotional fatigue would often envelop me within an hour or two—thus leaving me extremely exhausted and totally burned out for the remainder of the school day.

Now that I was determined to retire, I began to take a retroactive view of what I had done during the years of my youthfulness. For the most part, I had spent the equivalent of thirty years as a public servant. Most of these years were dedicated to public school teaching. Public school teachers often sacrifice their life and wage earnings for the benefit of the local community, the national society, and the global community. Undoubtedly, one can recognize and comprehend that I was a classroom teacher who viewed himself as an integral part of an educational system for the benefit of both the student clientele and public well-being of society. Now I knew that the time had come for me to let someone else carry the baton. I had taught for twenty-one years at Yuma High School. If my memory serves me well, I firmly stated in my exit report, "It is enough."

Chapter 10

People of Influence

When I originated on the plains of the Cape Fear River Basin of eastern North Carolina, there were already generational individuals who were role models. These individuals, though not all of them, were often extended relatives who were well respected within the community. Pulsating in their charismatic lifestyles were moral and social standards that influenced the entire community. These individuals of integrity were like mountainous lights, role models who were viewed by the entire community. They were the influential and precious ones who impacted me as well. Listed below are some of the names of these influential souls.

Many admired my paternal grandparents, Clint Smith and Sylvia Darden Smith. I first learned from my daddy that Grandfather Smith was in the shingle business. Later, in my adult years, Uncle Rayford, one of Daddy's older brothers, corroborated what Daddy had disclosed. Uncle Rayford further stated that when he was approximately thirteen or fourteen years old, he said to my grandfather Smith that there was more money in logs than in shingles. Based on Uncle Rayford's influence, my grandfather shifted his entrepreneurship from shingling to logging. In addition to his entrepreneurship, Grandfather was an ardent proponent for social values that publicly benefited the community. Meanwhile, according to a valid source, Grandmother Smith worked very hard at home, manning and maintaining the farm.

Next were my maternal grandparents, Richard Bryant and Mary Foy Bryant. Grandfather Richard was an astute farmer. Unlike most tenant farmers or sharecroppers, he farmed on a third. For example, his landowner only required one-third receipt of his cash crops. Moreover, my grandfather Richard had an upgraded riding plow. This agricultural implement on which he rode was drawn by a team of mules. Sometimes he would even let my brother Earl and me ride along with him. He was also an early seasonable planter and transplanter. Knowing these agricultural skills and when to implement them is what accounted for Granddaddy's success as a farmer. My grandmother Mary was an herbal apothecary. She was gifted in collecting a variety of herbs and other essential substances that would cure or heal certain diseases. European and Black Americans throughout the county would come to my grandparents' residence for Grandmother's healing medicine. Those who were not immediately healed, upon following my grandmother's instruction, later reported the evidence of healing in their bodies. Even Daddy utilized my grandmother's herbal medication. Daddy disclosed that, as a young man, he was afflicted with hemorrhoids. He stated that he revealed his painful condition to "Mrs. Mary." Afterward, my grandmother Mary made him a salve and gave him instructions concerning its application to the area. He said he was never again bothered with hemorrhoids. Perhaps Daddy said it best: "Mrs. Mary was a good woman."

Next in line were Perry Miller and Ida Bryant Miller. Uncle Perry and Aunt Ida were pillars of uprightness, whose ideal marriage gained the respect of the community. They lived in prosperity and with moral and social integrity. Uncle Perry and Aunt Ida were the first, whom I learned and knew, who set apart a tenth of their agricultural production as a tithe unto the Lord. Their dedication and faithfulness to this cause had a tremendous impact upon me, even now in the twenty-first century. Uncle Perry and Aunt Ida's name, impact, and legacy are still resonating in the local community: Perry Miller Road is named in their honor. Their eldest daughter, Cousin Elizabeth, was and still is a well-known preacher of righteousness in the community and region. Cousin Elizabeth's oldest son, Mr. William Gillespie (the grandson of Uncle Perry and Aunt Ida), was the principal of James Kenan High School for a number of years. Yes, I still refer to Mr. Gillespie as "Brother," (his nickname) for he is indeed my brother.

Two other people of influence were Cousin Hall McIver and Cousin Rebecca McIver. Here, it is prudent to point out that Cousin Rebecca's maiden name is to the same as Cousin Hall's surname; they were not related to each other before matrimony. Cousin Hall and Cousin Rebecca were among the most hospitable people I have ever known. Their home, according to a reliable source, was open to strangers, whom they received and dined. Their home was an open house to the neighborhood's adolescents as well. My brothers and I would frequent Cousin Hall and Cousin Rebecca's home, as did other teenagers. She had an uncanny capacity to relate and to communicate with teenagers. She would laugh and interact with us and enjoyed our presence and visitation as much as we teenagers did. Prior to our departure, Cousin Rebecca would always serve us delicious continental cuisine.

Moreover, they both embraced the principles of the Holy Writ, which invigorated their lifestyle. Their prosperity and enviable influence permeated the entire community.

Mr. O'Berry Miller and Mrs. Docia McGee Miller were also very important citizens of the community. They were early seasonal farmers, highly skilled in soil preparation and cultivation. Mr. O'Berry knew the time and season to transplant and plant certain crops. With their agricultural skills and ingenuity, along with heaven's blessings, they prospered immensely in crop production. In addition, Mr. O'Berry was among some of the first Black Americans who owned a tractor in the neighborhood. Another technical implement that the couple owned and operated was a sugarcane processor. After we harvested our sugarcane, Daddy would transport it to Mr. O'Berry, who would place the cane in his technical apparatus and extract the juice from the sugarcane. The sweet liquid was placed in a vat, where it was heated and cooked until it became a delectable taste to the client. One could not find a better-tasting molasses than a well-refined home-made one. Afterward, the molasses was poured into jars or containers, according to the client's specification.

Another great influence was Aunt Henrietta McIver McGowan. Oral history discloses that Aunt Henrietta was first married to my great uncle, who was my grandfather Richard Bryant's maternal uncle. Following the death of my great uncle, Aunt Henrietta later married Cousin John W. McGowan, Cousin Nathan McGowan's father. She was one who invested in the nation's richest and most precious resource: assisting and maintaining a vital stability of newborn infants. This is to say that Aunt Henrietta was a well-known practicing midwife throughout the community. Within Duplin County, North Carolina, her practical skills were utilized in the delivery of many human souls—both Black and White babies. Based on maternal sources, she was an integral part of the delivery team when I arrived on Earth. Full of wisdom, Aunt Henrietta was admired for her holy lifestyle. She was a sanctuary of praise and worship to God.

Cousin Armittie Miller was an astonishing woman, remarkable, and strong in character. Despite being a widow, she maintained the support and the stability of her family with great determination and perseverance. She endured the hardships and battled with being persistent to sustain herself and her children. A monumental pillar of the Church and of the neighborhood, Cousin Armittie was direct and straightforward in her manner of conduct and communication.

In those days, professional educators were heralded as typical role models; however, at work were other communal role models. The personnel at Garris Funeral Home in Mount Olive, North Carolina, had a unique way of investing in the youth. Rev. Robert Wallace and Mr. Robert Brimmage and Mr. Walter Barfield were the operators of the funeral establishment, under the ownership of Mr. Garris. As teenagers, my brothers, my first cousin, and I would often frequent the funeral home. The personnel treated us very well and always welcomed our presence. They would take us to make removals, take us on church funerals, take us to graveside services, and so forth. The cumulative effects of their professionalism and entrepreneurship and leadership abilities had an enormous impact upon me. It was from these experiences that I first entertained the notion of becoming an embalmer and funeral director. (A detailed account discloses my experience as a student and an apprentice of mortuary science in *The Sharecropper's Son*.)

Worthy People Who Helped

Interestingly, as I first pursued a degree in social science, there were several individuals who supported my cause. As was needed, these individuals willingly became available to help advance my progress. They were the ones whose hands and minds helped me to succeed in the aforementioned studies. With these words, let me personate each distinctive individual and their spouses: my brother Willie and his wife Zenobia Miller Smith; my brother Earl and his wife Dorothy King Smith; and Brother Donovan and his wife Clementine Smith McIntosh, who is my sister.

My brother Willie was the one who kept Betsy mechanically sound. If he was unable to repair Betsy, he always knew best which automobile shop or whom to recommend. He was a reliable, top-notch mechanic. To put it succinctly, his mechanical skills and expertise attained high marks.

Prior to his marriage to Dorothy King, my brother Earl lived in a boarding accommodation in the city of Middletown, New York. Mechanicstown was the area in which the boarding house was located. Earl, in his generosity and consideration, for the first time gave me a key to his room. After completing a day's work in the vicinity of that part of Orange County, I could go to his room and lie down and rest before attending evening classes at Orange County Community College (OCCC). In those days, I worked full time and attended evening classes twice a week for three hours per class. After class, I would drive home to Newburgh.

Soon Earl and Dorothy were united in matrimony. The newlyweds moved into an apartment within the city of Middletown, New York until they purchased their own private dwelling at One Vincent Drive. In each residence, they favored me with a key and hearty welcome to their lovely home. Many times when I arrived for the purpose of attending evening classes, home-cooked meals were already prepared. I would eat to my delight, rest comfortably, and attend evening classes from 7 to 10 PM. Earl and Dorothy's hospitality continued until I graduated from OCCC. Sometime after I had arrived in Tucson, I returned their key by mail.

Brother Donovan McIntosh and his wife, Clementine Smith McIntosh were tremendously helpful. Brother Donovan (Don) was not only helpful in a literate way but served as a mechanic for my car. He would tune up Betsy. Together, Brother Donovan and Clementine (Clem) were profoundly concerned that I would succeed in higher education. On my behalf, Brother Don and Clem's tutorial services included the following: suggestive and creative writing, organizational research and language synthesis, analytical research and brainstorming, and so forth. Their imparting expertise was the foundation that helped me to better focus on the practicality of expressive writing. Their help paved the way to a more excellent level of writing and understanding that was most accepted on the part of college professors.

Chapter 11

A Reflection

From the plains of the Cape Fear River Basin in rural eastern North Carolina to the southern tier of New York, where one can readily view the mountains and the slopes of the Hudson Valley, and to the valley floor and the tableland of the Sonoran Desert in southern Arizona is where I found a place to nestle. With my family, I first settled in Tucson, but later relocated to Yuma, Arizona. Strategically located, the Colorado River is flanked to the north and south of Yuma. To the South of Yuma, the territorial boundary of the United States is the nation of Mexico. The citizens of Mexico are our southern neighbors. Moreover, Yuma is the access route of international trade to all points east, west, north, and south within the United States and its Central and South American nations.

Interestingly, southern Arizona is lavishly rich with natural resources. The greatest of these resources is solar energy: the sun. Other natural resources include gold, silver, copper, minerals, a variety of crops, cattle, and citrus products, to mention a few. On a higher plane, human souls, a plethora of Arizonan citizenry, are still the most precious and priceless resources. The state of Arizona illustrated this viewpoint. When I relocated to southern Arizona in 1974, I was fortunate enough to qualify for scholarships and other financial aid. In reality, the Arizona desert was the Promised Land. I enrolled at the University of Arizona with a direct sense of purpose. I earned two degrees, a bachelor's and later a master's degree. I was smitten with the action of learning. This eventually led me to serve in the public sector of education. In the face of circumstances, I prevailed and influenced many people. Therefore, let it be resounded that education is the door of superabundance for the current generation and for future generations. President Barack Obama pointed out that education is not an option but is mandatory.

Chapter 12

My Mother's Final Days: A Transition

In my first book, *The Sharecropper's Son,* I mentioned in my dedication that Mother is still with us. This dear lady was once a vivacious and vibrant person, and remained that way for several decades. Unfortunately, her children and family members, friends, and acquaintances have observed Mother as being in her declining season. Still, in all probability, most of us parents do not necessarily expect to outlive our children. Yet Mother has seen two of her sons laid to rest: first Willie, who died February 26, 2000, and then Earl, who died June 23, 2006. As evidenced, life is transitory. One day the whole of humankind will make that transition, each according to his appointed time. Mother is now suffering from

Alzheimer's. It is just a matter of time, and her children are standing with her to the very end of her days. Mother, you have served us exceedingly well. You have fought a good fight.

About the Author

The oldest of seven children, Samuel Smith, Jr. began his journey more than sixty years ago in Kenansville, North Carolina. After graduation in 1961, he headed to Newburgh, New York. There he married and had a son. After thirteen years in New York, he moved to Tucson, Arizona, then to Yuma, Arizona. He taught high school social studies in Yuma for twenty-one years and retired in 1997.

Samuel's academic preparations include a Certificate of Graduation in mortuary science from McAllister Academy Institute of Funeral Services, New York City (1963); A.A. in social science from Orange County Community College, Middletown, New York (1974); B.A. in education from the University of Arizona in Tucson, Arizona in 1976; and an M.T. in education from the University of Arizona (1979). He pursued further studies at Trinity College in Washington, D.C. and California Polytechnic State University at San Luis Obispo. Samuel also served two years in the U.S. Army (one year in Viet Nam) (1966-1968). An ordained minister through The

Church of God in Christ in 1965, Samuel ministers in his travels and ministers at a local R.V. park. Samuel is a licensed embalmer and funeral director in the states of New York and Arizona, and has received of recognition in the field of education and ministry.

LaVergne, TN USA
03 March 2010
174723LV00001B/4/P